I'd Lose My Soul to a Chocolate Malt...

and other stories of everyday spirituality

Mike Tighe

One Liguori Drive
Liguori, Missouri 63057-9999
(314) 464-2500

*"Dedicated to the people
who have been Christ to me, even when
I haven't realized it at the time."*

M.T.

Imprimi Potest:
William A. Nugent, C.SS.R.
Provincial, St. Louis Province
The Redemptorists

Imprimatur:
Monsignor Maurice F. Byrne
Vice Chancellor, Archdiocese of St. Louis

ISBN 0-89243-316-7
Library of Congress Catalog Card Number: 89-63837

Copyright © 1990, Mike Tighe
Printed in U.S.A.

All rights reserved. No part of this book may be reproduced, stored in a retrieval system, or transmitted without the written permission of Liguori Publications.

Scripture texts used are taken from THE NEW AMERICAN BIBLE WITH THE REVISED NEW TESTAMENT, copyright © 1986, by the Confraternity of Christian Doctrine, Washington, DC 20005, and are used with permission. All rights reserved.

Cover and interior art: Chris Sharp

Table of Contents

PROLOGUE 5

GETTING TO KNOW GOD
   How Like Squirrels We Are 10
   Bringing God Out of the Closet 14
   Rediscovering God 17
   Living the Message of the Our Father 20
   Going One-on-one With God 24
   Placing More Faith in God's Son and in His Sun 27

SEEING GOD THROUGH FAMILY AND FRIENDS
   My Children Taught Me Well 32
   People Are Sacraments Too 37
   Waiting for a Call 40
   "Stupid" Galatians! 42
   Thank You, Mr. Duggan and Uncle Frank 46
   I Chased My Son and Caught Myself 50
   Spending More Time With the Family 53
   Let Go and Let Drive 57

RECALLING THE GOD OF THE PAST
    Bad Old Days — or Good Old Days? 62
    Lent Yesterday and Lent Today 65
    I Was Afraid I'd Lose My Soul to a Chocolate Malt 68

MEETING GOD THROUGH RANDOM REFLECTIONS
    Is There Life After Hockey? 73
    Warning: Bumps Ahead 76
    Jousting at Dirt Hills 78
    Finding Christ Everywhere 82
    Empty Trays, Empty Lives 86
    John 3:16 and Romans 10:9 88
    That One-more Syndrome 90

EPILOGUE 93

Prologue

Theologians — God love them — often make the process of trying to learn about God too complicated. And their complex notions often make it more difficult to meet Christ in life as well. Now, don't get me wrong. I don't dislike theologians. In fact some of my best friends are theologians. Their insights often prove helpful, so they do serve a useful purpose on earth. I just thank heaven that I don't have to spend so much of my time searching through books to gain a better understanding of God when it's so easy to meet him in daily life.

I discovered the complexities of theological thinking and writing when I turned in my first paper en route to a master's degree in theology. I'm not the most cerebral thinker in the world, so the research and writing were difficult tasks. But I thought that the paper, on a topic I've long since forgotten, was more than adequate. I expected a "C" at least, or perhaps a "B."

Imagine my surprise when the professor returned the paper with a large red "F" emblazoned on the top. But his rationale was even more surprising. He said he'd given me that grade because the paper read too much like a newspaper story. The sentences were too short and the paragraphs too brief for his taste.

I told him that was a natural writing pattern for me, a newspaper journalist. He countered that this was theology, not journalism. So

I went home, set my margins a little wider, and proceeded to retype the paper. Notice that I didn't say "rewrite." I just retyped it — merely changing simple sentences into complex ones and complex ones into compound-complex structures. Of course, I also ran my small paragraphs into large ones so that some took up almost a full page. I found the proofreading difficult as I struggled to understand the wordy sentences and lengthy paragraphs that I had grasped quite easily in their shorter form. (Perhaps anyone who has read a theological tract will understand what I mean.)

While I personally thought the effort reduced my work to a complicated mess, the professor thought it was much improved — so much so, in fact, that he gave me a "B," even after a slight deduction because it was a second try.

Another time during my journey toward a master's degree, I was having a horrible time understanding a particularly tedious concept that needed explanation in an oral presentation. So I figured out an easy way to explain it to myself, using illustrations of airplane parts. These were practical things I could understand. Unfortunately, I also used them during my presentation and virtually the entire class hooted and howled at me. One commented that the presentation simply wasn't erudite enough.

I hope it's easy to see why I believe that theologians often make things too hard. Oh, I'm not saying that understanding God is easy. Indeed, even with all the study, many facets remain a mystery. But I can't buy into making things complex just so they appear difficult enough to impress someone.

However, it wasn't until many years after those postgraduate days that it became clear that God doesn't necessarily speak to us in complex thoughts, long sentences, and ponderous paragraphs. God doesn't use a bullhorn to communicate with us. Rather, he's more likely to speak in whispers. He rarely appears as a pillar of flame like he did in the Old Testament. Instead, he's more prone to enter our lives as a spark and let us nurture the flame. He usually doesn't strike us blind, as he did Saint Paul. Rather, he nudges us gently, leaving the decision of action up to us. In short, when we look for a loud, dramatic, or forceful sign of God's presence in our lives, we may be as disappointed as a young child struggling to ward off the sandman to catch a glimpse of Santa Claus.

Luckily, we're not all theologians who have to struggle with knowing *about* God. Our task is to try to *know* God personally. That can have its difficult moments as well, and at least the theologians' background efforts can help sometimes. Perhaps just as importantly, we discover God's messages, signals, and presence each day of our lives — within ourselves and through others. They are there to help us to know God, if we stop long enough to listen, watch, and feel that presence.

We have to be aware of those simple opportunities for God to enter our lives so we can take advantage of them. Often these messages are as close as Christ's dwelling in the person sitting next to us, whether a spouse or child at home, a friend or a coworker, or a stranger we meet. Christ is present in these people, talking through them, showing us how to live a stronger faith life, perhaps pushing us to actions that will help us or others. We have to be aware of others' actions, touches, and signals to be able to receive these messages. And the messages can come from lifeless objects as well during a reflective moment.

These reflections exemplify the presence of God, Christ, and the Spirit in daily life — like experiencing a warm and loving hug from Christ through the arms of a normally standoffish teenager; or watching the frantic activities of a hungry squirrel searching for food, and realizing that's the way we often act toward our God. A spiritual message can come from something as innocuous as an empty ice-cube tray, if we're observant and open. Another can come from the bottom up — from children to adults — instead of from the top down, as most adults are more accustomed to and comfortable with. A message can evolve from a negative incident as well as a positive one.

This book follows a simple format; each chapter can be read independently. You can just read one if you're short on time or in a reflective mood; or you can read several if you have more leisure on another day.

Openness to looking for Christ in family, in friends, and in strangers is essential to these often delightful, although sometimes heavy and thought-provoking, discoveries. I haven't always been attuned to such openness. Even now that I'm aware of its benefits, I'm sure I still miss most of the messages sent my way. But I've found that the search helps me discover new things about myself, as well as about Christ's continuing action in this world. Like so many others, I often spend so much time waiting for the Second Coming that I forget Christ walks with me, in myself, and in others every day.

Getting to Know God

How Like Squirrels We Are

The squirrel approached cautiously, as was his habit, tentatively advancing three bounds, then retreating two. His daily foray for bread scraps on our deck was predictable: He'd scout the terrain, make sure nobody was stirring in the kitchen, then cautiously edge toward the bread. The slightest move in the kitchen would send him scampering at least to the edge of the steps and often down them until it looked safe enough to pursue his mission anew.

Sometimes when my wife, Susan, and I persisted in our morning routine of eating breakfast and preparing lunches, he'd be so bold as to risk capture. He'd streak toward the bread, scoop it into his chubby cheeks, and beat a hasty retreat to eat it in relative safety, perched on his favorite fencepost.

Eventually, the squirrel developed enough faith in our reliability at putting out the crumbs that he also started trusting us to some degree. He'd even allow one of us to stand on the deck — at an appropriate distance, of course, and he was the judge of that — while he retrieved his daily morsels and scampered away to hide them for safekeeping. He never did develop a level of confidence that would allow us to actually hand him a piece of bread, although we did try.

The squirrel would give us a second chance when we forgot to put out the bread, backing off into the yard while we did the scrambling to break up the bread and toss it out to him. But he was even more cautious on those days and took his own sweet time about collecting the loot, often waiting until we were gone from the house.

One day, when we'd forgotten to put out his daily bread, I decided to sit inside, sip my coffee, and observe how he'd react. I fully expected him to rummage around the deck for a few moments, then depart. Imagine my surprise when our gray, furry friend instead approached the door, sat on his hind legs, and cocked his head quizzically one way, then the other. He then tiptoed to the spot where the bread normally lay and pawed at the gray decking. He returned to the door and stared at me intently, occasionally glancing back at where he'd expected his stash to be. He gingerly stood on his hind legs and placed his tiny paws on the screen. Slowly at first, then with more intensity, he scratched at the screen.

He was begging! I thought that maybe we'd broken the final barrier of mistrust and gained a friendly pet who actually would try to communicate with us. Slowly, ever so slowly, I edged toward the cupboard and delicately pulled a piece of bread from the plastic bag touting the bread's butter top and enriching qualities. I tiptoed to the door and cautiously slid it open enough to squeeze my hand out.

The squirrel skittered away at the noise of the door, but settled about four feet away and looked back. I extended my hand with the bread, but he backed up farther, his tail rapidly furling and unfurling. I nudged the bread forward; he crept backward. I pulled back; he advanced. Finally, late for work, I realized that I wouldn't be able to coax the squirrel to take the bread from my hand, so I just dropped it on the deck and left. As I drove away, I noticed him prancing across the lawn, bread grasped firmly in his jowls.

The squirrel didn't return the next day or the next or the next, as our offerings of bread hardened in the sun one day, became a soggy mess because of a rain shower on the next, and finally were swept away in gusts of wind. I figured the squirrel had become impatient with us and found another "patsy" for his panhandling ways. About two weeks later I noticed him approaching stealthily again. He perched on his fencepost, surveyed the the deck, saw no bread, and left.

As I pondered our relationship with this creature, it dawned on me that it resembled the way we humans often act toward God. Rather than believing what we've been taught — that God is approachable and, indeed, longs for us to interact with him — we often are as insecure and skittish as this squirrel. We want God to help us, and we ask him to do so, but we try not to get too close. Often we relegate our entreaties to weekends, and only in church, but we rarely invite God confidently into our daily lives.

As long as our lives are going smoothly, and it appears that God is giving us our daily bread, we see no reason to develop a closer relationship with him. We advance cautiously, accept his offering, and retreat to the comfort and security of our families, our homes, and our jobs.

But when something goes wrong, we suddenly become emboldened like the squirrel, scratching on God's door and begging for help with this problem or that difficulty. We've been getting what we want without committing ourselves, and we start believing that it's our right. We retreat rapidly when God extends a helping hand but asks for a commitment from us at the same time. Or, if we don't get exactly the answer we want, we impatiently withdraw from God altogether, looking for help from someone else or finding solace in something else. Like the squirrel, we may look from afar, but we hesitate to approach for fear that we'll have to commit to something.

While it's true that God offers unconditional love, it's also true that the Christian message is to commit ourselves to a relationship with our Christ, our God, our Spirit. And we're duty-bound to foster this message, helping one another and working to build community. We're not to live as independently as squirrels, cautiously taking but never freely giving, selfishly hiding our walnuts and fruits and morsels of bread, only to wonder later where we might have stashed some of them. (Watch a squirrel some winter day, feverishly digging in the snow, frantically looking for nuts he'd hidden so carefully only a few months before.)

Rather, we're to work with God to build a two-way relationship with him, listening as much or more than just asking and talking, and working with one another to spread the fruits of that relationship. Our relationship with God blossoms as we work to become comfortable with it and spread its benefits.

We're to become less squirrellike, more settled, more confident, more giving. It's then that we receive — and there's no need to beg.

Bringing God Out of the Closet

I remember spending much of one afternoon when I was just a young lad trying to get God to come out of the closet.

We'd just learned in school that God is everywhere, that he sees all and knows all. Sister said he's even in closets, and he can even see in the dark. I wasn't very theologically astute at the time — and only rarely am even now — so I decided to test the theory at home. I figured that if I jerked the closet door open real fast, I'd be able to see God before he disappeared from sight. Well I nearly wore the door off its hinges, coming up with nothing but air. I even went into the closet one time and closed the door, figuring God would talk to me even if I couldn't see him. All that did was scare the daylights out of me, as I imagined goblins and ghoulies surrounding me, but no God.

Unfortunately, the "God-is-everywhere" imagery of those days focused on negative reasoning instead of the positive. God wasn't seen as being everywhere to be helpful but, rather, to be vengeful when we crossed him. The common message — at least the one we heard, even if a more friendly one was intended — was that God is everywhere, and he sees everything we do, especially the bad things. When we made mistakes, there was nowhere to run, nowhere to hide. He'd even find us in a closet, just as he found Adam and Eve cowering in the Garden.

Of course, we also learned that we're on earth to "know, love, and serve God in this world, and be happy with him in the next." But how could we get to know someone who scared us to death? And how could we imagine being happy with someone in the next world when all he was interested in was tracking us down and punishing us in this one?

Now, however, God's out of the closet. He's not a mean old curmudgeon interested only in tripping us up, but a gentle, loving being who wants us to grow in love of him and of one another. The images of an icy, angry God have melted into visions of a warm, helpful one — one who has sensitive, feeling characteristics that are more inviting and comforting.

We're beginning to replace the many Old Testament images of God who is often depicted as a punishing character in his dealings with Israel with images of him as one who is warm and protective. We're also adding our own ideas of God the Father, Christ, and the Holy Spirit to what we learned in our catechism days: that we're created in God's image and likeness.

The varying images of God that are being touted today, including a God with feminine characteristics, often prompt debates over theological interpretations. But they also provide opportunities for deep reflection. Exploring these images with one another can enhance our understanding of the deity, if we're open enough to discuss them. For instance, rarely do we need an image of a temperamental, punishing God, and we can learn little from it. While fear of the Lord can be — indeed, was and sometimes still is — an effective motivator, love of the Lord can accomplish much more in much less time and with much more far-reaching results. We need an understanding God, not one who won't listen. We need a comforting one, not one who ignores us in our time of trouble.

And sometimes, we need a feminine God, to enhance our own understanding of God and of one another.

Some moderns choose varied wording for the Sign of the Cross, with one of the more popular versions being "In the name of the Creator, and the Redeemer, and the Sanctifier." That one sparks more fiery debate than the heat from the pillar of fire in the Old Testament. There will be no attempt here to resolve the debate, as it would take volumes of books and hours of discussion to bridge the gap between the two camps. And even then, it's certain that not everyone would be satisfied.

Basically, the discussion hinges on theological meaning. It's hard to argue with the fact that each Person of the Trinity does, indeed, accomplish the task attributed. But the argument for the traditional format keys on the relationships of the three Persons, which proponents maintain must remain Father, Son, and Spirit to maintain one of the basic tenets of our faith.

That issue is pointed out here merely for reflection and discussion. By bringing God out of the closet we can learn a lot by exploring all the various images applied to him.

Rediscovering God

I think I'm like most people in feeling a tad insecure when moving to new surroundings. I especially felt that way when my job change forced my family and me to move to another city, and I located there about five months before the rest of the family did.

I moved from a job where I'd earned the professional respect of my coworkers and the community, if not the newspaper's management. I was leaving a city where strong Church ties had seen me involved in numerous parish activities, and I was now going to go to a much larger city where I would start as a nameless face in the pew. My wife, Susan, was being torn from her native city, her friends, and her job. The kids were leaving the only school they ever attended and the only neighborhood they'd ever known to try to fit into a new school in a strange neighborhood.

Those feelings and questions about whether the job I'd be starting the next day would work out contributed to a lonely feeling that first night in the sleeping room I'd rented until my family would join me. It was bad enough missing family and friends without having to stare at those stark bare walls. There was nothing to establish my identity as a person. I spent much of that night, and several subsequent nights, trying to rectify that. Slowly and with care, I hung photos here, placed trinkets there, and distributed a small collection of hats throughout the room to show myself that I belonged there if my belongings did — all this to establish my existence there.

I felt somewhat at home when the project was completed, although there's no way to duplicate the sounds of the kids laughing, running through the house as if it were a gym or bickering over some senseless thing. I was lonely, but I was declaring my turf, reassuring myself, trying to overcome that loneliness.

Reflecting on how unsettled I was until I had that territory — my territory — established, I wondered whether Christ becomes frustrated with people who fail to respond when he invites them to join him on *his* turf, to help make the Christian community whole, to restore its identity. I also wondered why some persons are called early in life and never waver, while others never respond at all. It finally dawned on me that it's not a matter of Christ's calling at different times. He calls all the time. But the key is when people hear and when they answer. Sometimes they hear but postpone answering.

Christ waits as his creatures hover somewhere between an early response and no response. Perhaps his vigil is a calm one, perhaps an anxious one, maybe an impatient one. There was a long period in my life when I must have tried his patience, finding reasons not to answer. I thought instead that I could get along without religion, without the community of believers. I didn't have time for the Church; sleep was more important. I used the common line that I really didn't need the institutional Church, the four stone walls, all the trappings. I could talk to God, to Christ, to the Spirit, anytime and anywhere I wanted. Of course, the only problem was that I parroted that line but didn't follow through on it. I rarely talked to any of them, and I never really listened either.

Unfortunately, in cutting myself off from God, I often missed the opportunities to meet him through other people as well. I wasn't seeking him anywhere, let alone in other people. Looking back now, I can count several times when he was calling through other people, but I was too dense to realize it. Happily, I've returned to the community during the past ten years or so. As is often the case, my children were one of the instruments. I thought I'd better get my act together and become a better example to them. At first I started going to church again mechanically, with little real thought about what was happening. But, as time went on, I also became involved in various church and school activities, and enjoyed the community. A retreat weekend several years ago helped me work even more into the community.

Now, don't get the wrong impression. I'm not a saint by any means. I still often balk when Christ wants me to stay on his turf. I'm sure I still try his patience many times. But I've rediscovered the importance of the community of believers and the need for personal action to bring Christ's message into daily life so that all people may enter into God's life.

But probably most important, I think I've become a better listener so I'm not quite as startled when I feel Christ tapping on my shoulder. And I feel much less lonely now that I have rediscovered him.

Living the Message of the Our Father

Many people were shattered when certain theologians announced that their studies indicate Christ didn't compose the Our Father. The scholars said the prayer contains phrases similar to those Christ would have used, but that early Christian communities actually formulated the prayer as it is recorded in the Bible.

Some were devastated, and their faith was shaken. Others dismissed the idea, contending that the theologians were trying to undermine Christ, belittle the churches, and erode people's faith. But many others opted for a more faith-filled response. "So what?" they asked. So what if Christ didn't compose the prayer the night before on his personal computer, run it past his Father, and then pass it out to climax his Sermon on the Mount? The point is that Christ created a mood, a message so intense that his followers were able to paraphrase his ideas into such a beautiful and all-encompassing prayer that it has weathered the centuries to remain unchallenged as the perfect prayer.

The book-wormish scholars will continue in their quest to nail down precisely the historical Jesus, to discover exactly what Christ the man did and did not do; but what is important for us is the *presence* of Jesus in our midst. Thankfully, not many of us are qualified for this type of intellectual, letter-of-the-law study of religion. But we can be grateful to those who study in this way because they leave us the luxury of getting to know Christ the Person better.

Jesus' presence has left a legacy — regardless of whether or not he actually composed the Our Father. And that legacy continues today through Christ's presence in each of us. Unfortunately, we remember that concept only when it comes up during a sermon at Mass. Perhaps it lasts through the sign of peace, when we turn to our families and neighbors to wish them the peace of Christ. But amnesia often sets in even as the church door is closing behind us. We promptly forget that Christ is in us, let alone anyone else, as we dart to our cars so we can hurry up and wait to get out of the parking lot. And woe to those who try to cut in front, those who were images of Christ only minutes before!

Do we spend our Sundays treating ourselves and our families and friends as if Christ dwells in each, or do we rush out to shop or hurry home to languish in front of the TV for the rest of the day? If we actually do live our Sundays with Christ, do we tuck that concept away for a week when we go to bed Sunday night, or do we take it to work and play with us throughout the week? Do we act like we really believe that Christ lives in each of us, or do we merely mouth those words out of habit?

If we believed — *really* believed — that Christ is in each of us, we would show far more respect for one another. Oddly enough, we're often the least Christian to those in our own families. Few sayings are so true as the one that if we treated our friends like we do our children, we wouldn't have any friends.

I'd have to confess that this is one of my weakest points. I could preach up a storm about it, about the need to be Christian in the home and treat one another with respect and kindness, then go home and go BOOM when one of the kids lights my all-too-short fuse. All my words of wisdom and intellectual understanding of the concept disappear in a mushroom of smoke as I lose my temper and go toe-to-toe with one of the kids. Every time I think I've got my temper under control, I backslide and wonder why I've shut Christ out. It's a continuing struggle. But overcoming it is rewarding when a conflict arises and I manage to control my angry feelings and remind myself that I'm dealing with another person in whom Christ lives, and then act accordingly.

But again, if we all *really* believed what we are taught and what we ourselves preach, wouldn't there be less honking and more yielding the right of way when driving? Wouldn't there be less hoarding and more sharing with the poor and homeless? Wouldn't there be less stubbornness and more openness in settling our conflicts with one another? Wouldn't there be less war, more peace?

All this should start in the morning when we look in the bathroom mirror, somehow recognizing Christ behind the stubble or smeared makeup on our faces, and begin the day with a hearty "hi" to him in us. After beginning the day with a "hi" to ourselves and the Christ in us, it would be a good idea to say or wave "hi" often throughout the day. It doesn't hurt one iota to say "hi" to the Christ in friends, neighbors, and strangers — maybe most importantly to strangers. (Besides, it's kind of fun to see how startled some people are when a stranger says "hi." And they often pass it on.)

We have to get beyond just saying that Christ is with us, and begin to live it — from small matters like "hi" to large matters like promoting peace, working for social justice, and sharing our faith. We may be fooling ourselves if we're waiting for the Second Coming of Christ. What if, as some suggest, the Second Coming is now and he has to come through us? We're stuck here until we get it right. Who cares who composed the Our Father when what is more important is living its message?

Going One-on-one With God

Although it's true that we're not supposed to make our faith journeys alone, there's much to be said for going one-on-one with God as we go through life.

After all, we'll be meeting God alone, and the gang won't be there to put in a good word. Not to worry though — God isn't as intimidating as we sometimes have thought. In fact it's often far, far easier to deal with God and his simple guidelines than it is to interact with mere mortals and modern complex statutes. We know where we stand with God. Basically, all we have to do is stick to two rules: Love God above all things, and our neighbor as ourselves. All other actions can flow as easily from these two tenets as water from a faucet.

Many of us are old enough — or young enough, depending on how we're feeling on a particular day — to remember the tail end of the good old days when a lot of transactions were closed with a word or a handshake. Maybe, if really big bucks were involved, a contract might have had to be signed. But that paper didn't demand the signer's firstborn as collateral.

Such is not the case nowadays, as my family and I discovered when we moved to another city and built a house. Our first one had cost just a bit more than many cars cost these days. Oh, it needed plenty of work, but it eventually became our home; and we hated to part with it, especially when we went house shopping and couldn't find an affordable one to replace it.

So we opted to build. We dealt with a builder of the old-fashioned sort, with a verbal agreement here, a handshake there, and a phone call for change orders in between. Oh, a few missed communications eventually cost both us and the builder a little more money, but it was a comfortable relationship based on faith, trust, and one another's integrity.

But we weren't so fortunate with others! They presented hassles galore! Financial institutions wouldn't take our word for anything. We had to tell them the facts, verify the facts, then prove the verification of the facts. After that, they still wouldn't believe us, so we had to get somebody else write a letter to verify our proof of the verification of the facts. Then they told us we've got to have an attorney to make sure the facts were right, and the attorney told us that our casual relationship with the builder could put the whole deal in jeopardy.

Well, things eventually worked out for us, no thanks to human beings and computers and the quirky rules and regulations of each. But the process of proving ourselves worthy of making house payments for the rest of our lives is so degrading, so humiliating, and so frustrating that it contrasts sharply with the simple process we can follow to have a solid relationship with our God. Love him above all, and love our neighbor as ourselves.

First of all, if we follow those two rules there is no need for letters, proofs, or further verifications. Second, if we falter, we can reconcile matters between ourselves and God.

If we need — or think we need — something, just a prayer and a handshake will do. The prayer will be answered. Perhaps it won't be in the form we want, but we can have faith that it's being answered in some way.

Most likely the reasons we have enveloped ourselves in so much red tape and doubt of one another's integrity is that somebody, somewhere along the line, violated God's two simple rules. So we figured we needed laws, rules, and regulations to protect ourselves from one another.

We can be grateful that God isn't a bureaucrat, but trusting and trustworthy instead. Just a prayer and a handshake is enough. This one-on-one approach to God is better and much more lasting than any mortgage we could buy on earth. Besides, the interest rates are more than reasonable.

Placing More Faith in God's Son and in His Sun

T ime was, a lad who got his shoes wet in a creek would just pull them off, prop them up on a rock or a couple of sticks, and let the sun do the work of drying them out. Meanwhile there was always time to catch a few more fish.

A Norman Rockwell vision of such a scene crossed my mind recently when I saw two boys around age ten standing near the electric hot-air hand dryer in the restroom of a state park campground. The boys looked startled and sheepish when I walked in, so I figured that they might be up to a little mischief. But one of them grinned slowly and explained, haltingly, "Uh, fell in the crick, sir, and, uh, I'm dryin' my shoes off."

I nodded as I noticed him holding the shoes under the dryer. It appeared to me that he'd started a long, tedious process, if not a futile one that had to be explained to everyone who walked in. I asked why he didn't just leave the shoes out in the sun to dry.

"Naw," he said. "There's no breeze today. Plus, I don't want my Mom to find 'em."

I tried to explain that the sun might work better and more quickly, regardless of the lack of breeze. And Mom might even be less likely to find out, if that were a burning issue, which it might become on a certain part of his anatomy.

The Rockwell vision faded to thoughts of how similar the boys' actions were to the way we often are with God. We get in a jam and look to our own human-made contraptions for a solution instead of trusting in the hand of God to help. Like the boys, we choose technology over God's nature to try to improve our lot in life.

We treat our soil like dirt, over-fertilizing ground that had been doing just fine before our chemicals started crumbling its long-range productivity. Then, when we think we need still more production, we build larger, more powerful machines to plow more and more ground, only to defile that as well with hazardous chemicals. If we scoff at the idea that such chemicals are dangerous, why do we post signs on fertilized lawns warning that children and pets should not play on the grass for a certain number of days? It's not to protect the grass, but to shield the children and pets from the poison that rain soon enough will send into our groundwater and our rivers and streams.

We dam up and rechannel rivers to suit our whims, fancy, and fantasy, perhaps to make room for more development, perhaps because we think we can make it into a more efficient delivery system, or perhaps because we think we can improve our recreational opportunities. Never mind that God created rivers, their surroundings, and the wildlife they host with a delicate, interdependent balance. Without recognizing — or, perhaps, caring — that we may be creating nothing but a vast, rapid drainage ditch spewing sewage into the ocean, we build to suit our needs today, and tomorrow be damned.

When we're not rechanneling our water, we're often wasting it.

In the spring we wrestle our sprinklers out of the tangle of hoses in the garage even before temperatures are warm enough to stir plant life. Then we start watering to force the green. The watering doubles when a dry spell brings even a hint of brownness, even though experts say that watering then may not help a lawn and could hurt it. God had the wisdom to give grass the resiliency to live through a brown dormant stage without dying, but we mess with the system and upset the balance.

And oh, how we mistreat our forests, thoughtlessly chopping them down and bulldozing them away so we can continue the malling — you may also read *mauling* — of America from sea to shining sea. Then we bemoan the fact that a forest fire may reduce a stand of timber to kindling. We don't distinguish between a natural fire and a human-caused one, thinking foolishly that we, the smartest animals on earth, can bring the blazes back under our control. Later, we discover that fires are an integral part of nature and certain trees even have two kinds of seeds: regular and fireproof. The regular ones are for normal reseeding; the fireproof ones are God's ingenious little devices that allow him to reseed his garden after he's pruned the plants. We should not forget that this is *his* garden, and we're merely guests, intended to be stewards, not burglars.

This whole scenario brings to mind an anecdote I culled from a collection of an archbishop's favorite jokes and stories: A visitor walked up to a farmer relaxing on his porch. The visitor looked admiringly across the straight, weedless rows of corn, the gaily dancing fields of golden wheat, and the meticulously manicured lawn. "Golly, God does wonderful work, doesn't he?" the visitor asked.

"Yep," the farmer agreed, adding, "but you should've seen this place when he tried to do it all by himself."

Therein lies the rub: We don't appreciate the beauty of God's unsullied handiwork and think our work on this seventh day of creation will improve upon it. We can't accept the fact that maybe — just maybe — there's a happy medium to be found. We can coexist with nature, improving our lifestyles without harming God's creation. But we have to do it working with God and nature, not against him and it.

The youngster who was trying to dry his shoes with an electric hand dryer in the campground restroom is not to be blamed because hand dryers can control the problem of littering. But it's still an adjustment to see such a "human-made" convenience invading the great outdoors that God created with such care. It's almost as if we're afraid to get too far away from our own technology. But we cheat ourselves out of the pleasure of pure, unadulterated — dehumanized, in a positive sense — creation.

A little more faith in God's Son and his sun would do us more good than too much trust in our bulldozers, our chemicals, and other gadgetry.

Seeing God Through Family and Friends

My Children Taught Me Well

T he dreams of my youth often focused on the day when I'd become an adult and be able to quit learning things. "No more pencils, no more books..." became a theme song that was just as alluring for my future as a mother's lullaby had been comforting in my past.

Perhaps the most inviting thought, and one that helped me grapple with the growing pains of adolescence, was the fact that adults wouldn't be able to boss me around. No longer would I be shunted to the background, being seen and not heard, while they enjoyed their adult pursuits. In fact, if I became a parent myself, I'd have a chance to teach my own children a thing or two. Plus, I'd have ready-made dishwashers, lawn mowers, and snow shovelers to boot.

But I've awakened now and realized the error of my youthful dreams. I know now that learning not only is a lifelong process but also has changed to a bottom-up one in many respects. I've discovered that the kids teach me things as often as — sometimes more often than — I teach them. Sometimes they even teach me things about myself. For example, as I was cleaning up the kitchen after washing the dishes before I went out to mow the lawn one evening, I ran across a paper my son, Brendan, had brought home from school. The Christian action lesson was headed, "How I Look at Rules." The directions asked for the student's most important rules, the parents' most important rules, and a comparison of the two.

I hadn't seen the assignment before he did it and took it to school. But this completed and graded paper listed my rules as

- Get to work on time.
- Don't yell a lot.
- Act as a family driver at all times.

"Brendan!" I yelled, when I noticed that the assignment was to *ask* the parents what their rules are. "Where'd you get these rules for me?"

He ambled in and explained rather offhandedly that he'd forgotten to do the assignment at home so he'd made up the answers. "You didn't want me to have a late assignment, did you?" he asked innocently.

I muttered to myself about how the teacher must really wonder about my priorities, if those were my most important rules. Out loud I said, "Well, no, but I'd rather have you do it on time — and follow the directions." After a pause, honesty got the better of me and I confessed, "Then I could defend myself, and the teacher wouldn't get the wrong image of me."

Now, the truth was out. I was more concerned about what the teacher thought of me than I was about the image I'd been conveying to my family. Brendan put on his best pout — which, I might say, he learned quite well from me. Naturally, that stirred my guilt, as I realized that he'd merely written what he *perceived* to be my most important rules. He obviously observed my habits and extracted my rules from them.

I often give the kids a ride to school, but I'm usually yelling at them to hurry up so I won't be late for work. Then, when they yell at one another to get out of the bathroom or out of the way or whatever, I yell at them to quit yelling. Then we drive off to school like a bunch of grumpy, reluctant campers heading into a thunderstorm, often trying to figure out who will be needing a ride later in the day. I guess that maybe, once or twice, I may have mentioned that I feel like a gosh-darned — I suspect I used a stronger epithet — kiddie chauffeur.

I was not proud of what Brendan's assignment taught me that evening. It held a mirror up to me, and I was very uncomfortable with the image I was presenting to my family.

Brendan's not the only youthful teacher in the household. Even the youngest, Allison, often takes on a professorial tone. For example, the dinner-table discussion one night concerned whether or not a certain major purchase should be made. I can't even remember what item was at issue, but it probably was a VCR because that seems to prompt most of our family-spending arguments.

Allison didn't say much during the discussion. But at one point, without even looking up from her plate, the second grader said quite simply and nonchalantly, "Is it a need or a want?"

I was stunned, partly because I'd only recently heard of using that phrase to evaluate the necessity, legitimacy, and justice of spending money and partly because I was envious that she already knew it. Who was this young upstart to be teaching me a lesson? Allison's words of wisdom ended the discussion and the family went without whatever it was going to buy.

Not to be outdone, Annie, the oldest, is teaching me things constantly. Even though she's struggling with adolescence and its increasingly complex distractions and problems, she usually has a sensitive ear and sensible suggestion when asked to help sort out a problem. I find myself doing that often, as the blunt observations of a teenager often can cut through foggy confusion.

I'm also learning to adjust to her growing pains, which are quite different from those of my youth. For starters, the old seen-but-not-heard adage was quite true in my youth. Now teens are taught not only to have feelings but to express them. And they don't hesitate to exercise that vocal right. While that's probably a better option, it's also more complex and challenging than it was when I often lived in ignorant bliss of youthful problems.

It's also more challenging for a parent. I find I often have to sort out my own thoughts before I can offer help — if she wants it, which she often doesn't, and I have to adjust to that. It's also hard to keep up with teenagers' worries. I attended a parenting lecture during which the speaker confided that young people are most worried about nuclear war and parents ought to talk to them about it.

That night at supper, with a certain degree of self-satisfaction, I said to Annie, "What are you and your classmates most worried about?"

"Huh?" came the response, muffled in a mouthful of food.

"What thing absolutely concerns you the most, prompts the most worried discussions?" I asked, still confident that I was going to triumph in the role of teacher.

"AIDS," she said casually.

"Huh?" I said, nearly swallowing my tongue. I was dumbfounded, and my expression betrayed me.

"Oh, not because anybody's *doing* anything," she said, rolling her eyes in that parents-are-so-dumb facial contortion and evoking a sigh of relief on my part. "It's just that all the talk about it worries us."

Again, as the role-reversal continued, I was the pupil and a child was my teacher. Then I began to wonder when I would get my turn to be the teacher. The more I thought about it, the closer I came to the conclusion that the ultimate teacher — Jesus Christ — uses the children to continue the learning process of the parents. For sure, Christ is present in each of them and speaks through them, to those who have lost their childlike curiosity and faith.

From that perspective, I decided that I should offer a prayer of thanks to Christ for being present in these children and a prayer of petition to pay attention to the teachers.

I think I'm finally starting to learn.

People Are Sacraments Too

The concept of an eighth sacrament dawned slowly for me, but it was a bright ray when it pierced the clouds. While the first seven sacraments don't come to mind daily, at least their visible signs make them more obvious.

It took my oldest child to show me the light that people are sacraments too. Annie's a very complex person; her emotions run deep, but she likes to keep them under wraps. Oh, she'll give a hug now and then within the four walls of the house, but don't try to hug her in public. She'll reveal her hopes, her joys, and her disappointments when she's of a mind to, but she's likely to snap at those who try to pry when she's in a private, pensive mood.

Many people say Annie's got a lot of my traits. Unfortunately, those traits include a sharp, teasing tongue that often comes off as flip and uncaring, if not downright bitter. In fact, sometimes I get a little upset when I'm on the receiving end of her barbs. And the fact that she is (and I am) at the present time adjusting to her teen years makes for a potentially explosive combination. Yet she's an incredibly sensitive person who often knows just how to console people who seem troubled. (Some traits, apparently, she gets from her mother, and that's one of them.)

Annie's preparation to receive the sacrament of Confirmation included several projects at home, school, parish, and in the community at large. (Unfortunately, the service project didn't include picking up clothes in her room — or elsewhere in the house, for that matter — but that's a wholly different issue.) I observed the process with interest, and perhaps a degree of envy, because it was so different from my preparation for the sacrament. As I recall, what I thought about mainly before Confirmation was how hard the archbishop would "slug" me and how much fun it would be to be a valiant soldier of Christ. Images of armor and shields and being willing to die for the faith eventually disappeared as so much vapor.

Today the thrust is toward service as a Christian, a service orientation that confirmands are challenged to continue after they receive the sacrament.

I was surprised during the Confirmation Mass that I was getting a little more emotional than I'd expected. I was proud of Annie and the services she'd performed, but seeing her standing there straight and tall when she received the sacrament still sent an unexpected tingle up my spine.

After Mass she bounded up to me, and I asked for a hug. To my surprise and delight, she enthusiastically embraced me, in public, no less. Memories of her as a baby and youngster flashed across my mind, and the image of her smile burned itself into my brain. I was so stunned that it didn't occur to me until later that I'd actually held Christ in my arms for a fleeting moment. Reflecting on it later, I realized that I'd not only had flashes of her as she had been and was then, but I'd also been blessed with a vision of what she might become.

Since then I've watched her becoming, day by day. I've seen her on her "off" days, when she sometimes confides in me and we talk, and at other times when she clams up and journeys within herself.

And I've seen her on her "on" days, when she's bubbly and excited and filled with hope for the future. I appreciate her more now, no matter which day it is.

But I appreciate her most for those days when she continues to be a sacrament to me — Christ in the flesh — when I take the time to remember that and listen. She's helped me celebrate victories and overcome defeats. She's hugged me firmly when I'm happy and gently when I'm sad.

My daughter, Annie — an eighth sacrament, an outward sign instituted by Christ to give grace. I don't know why it didn't dawn on me before.

Waiting for a Call

I thought I was looking forward to the kids' being gone for a few weeks — until they were gone for a few hours.

Before they went to visit Grandma and Grandpa, I'd had dreams about how delightful the quiet would be. I'd be able to nap uninterrupted. I wouldn't be answering pleas for money to buy candy. I wouldn't hear the telltale noise of intense sibling rivalries escalating ever higher. And I wouldn't be yelling at them to pick up their toys and clothes, then picking them up myself.

Their plane had barely reached cruising altitude when I decided to treat myself to a fifteen-minute nap in my easy chair. I thought I might even be devilishly indulgent and take a full half-hour nap to recharge my batteries. Imagine my surprise and chagrin when I found myself tossing and turning, unable to get to sleep. The house was just too darned quiet.

As I listened for some sort of noise to remind me of normalcy, I even imagined welcoming Allison's hesitant touch and whisper, "Dad, can I have some ice cream?" (I also felt a tinge of guilt about the times I bit her head off when she had the gall to awaken me for such a nonemergency.) After a while, the intensity of listening so hard must have worn me out, and I nodded off.

During the next few days I found some aspects of the kids'

absence to be heavenly. There were few intrusive phone calls for the kids, so I didn't have to go out and look hither and yon to connect them with a friend. I didn't have to bus a group of kids to an activity, then pace my own activities so I'd be able to pick them up on time. There was no slamming front door, no tattling, and no fighting.

But I also found, as I had when I tried to take that first nap, that the loneliness quickly offset those small joys. It's been said that it's possible to be lonely, even in a crowd. I discovered how true that is, even in the middle of a huge shopping center, bustling with people searching for sales, or in a crowded church, rustling with bulletins being used as fans. Mere people don't seem to be enough company when I see other kids and wonder how *my* kids are doing.

As the empty days slowly, inexorably crept by, quite often I daydreamed about what the kids were doing at various times of the day. Were they fishing, swimming, canoeing, shopping, nursing a wound, quibbling with one another? Why didn't they call and say they were tired of their grandparents? Why didn't they phone and say they wanted to come home?

One evening, as I was rattling about the empty house, pouting about missing the kids, I wondered whether that might be how God feels sometimes, knocking around in that great big splendid heaven, waiting for his children's prayerful ring on the phone. After all, every person is a product of God's love; and — since it is customary to attribute human emotions to him — I suspect that loneliness is one of them.

Oh, I know that God doesn't pout about it, at least not like I pouted during the kids' vacation. And there are plenty of other souls to keep him company. I know that God can peek in on my life to see how I'm doing, even when I'm not communicating with him. But I wonder whether there aren't a lot of days and nights when he'd welcome a slamming door or a ringing phone or an interrupted nap from one of those special kids he hasn't heard from in quite some time.

"Stupid" Galatians!

People can cause untold damage to themselves and others when they blindly take a biblical passage out of context to suit their own purposes. Sometimes they even recast the phrasing ever so slightly so it underscores the point they're trying to make.

I recognize the danger, but nonetheless I am especially fond of the opening words of chapter 3 in Paul's Letter to the Galatians where he calls them "stupid." Paul is referring to something entirely different here, but I like the word because it tweaks my conscience when I botch up my life in any way. (It even comes to mind when I fly out on a 3-0 count with the bases loaded after my teammates in our "over-the-hill" softball league urge me to take a walk for the team.)

Oddly enough I ran across the verse during my first attempt at Bible study since leaving college. As it turned out the word "stupid" also described the effort our crew of six to ten men made as we studied the Bible. We had formed the group as a follow-up to a renewal weekend that focused on fostering Christian community.

At our first meeting we thought we'd better decide how to approach this study, which we undertook without guidance or outline. We opted to read a gospel a week and discuss it during our hour-long meeting.

Well, after a forty-five minute discussion of the Gospel of Mark, during which we figured we'd explored every nook and cranny of the work of this early Christian journalist, we were amazed at how simple this process of studying the Bible really was. "Why do people act like it's such a chore?" we asked one another with amazement. If we could do such a good job so quickly and so painlessly, why couldn't they? We expressed a good deal of sympathy for those others and then decided which gospel to discuss the following week.

We experienced the same results the next week and each succeeding week. Things were going so swimmingly that we never stopped to evaluate what we were doing or ask why it became easier for us to skip a week or two without feeling like we were missing anything. And Saint Paul called the Galatians "stupid"!

The fact is, we weren't really getting much out of our "stupid" approach to Bible study. But we were so wrapped up in the process of thinking we were studying that we didn't realize our process was flawed. And, when we became bored for lack of challenge, we abandoned our venture instead of asking for help. In short, we also abandoned one another when we didn't try a different tack.

Finally, however, we came to realize why some people spend their entire lives studying, perusing, and dissecting one short book of the Bible or even just a few verses from it. We started out like overconfident gangbusters but ended up skeptical about our ability to learn much more than a flip comment like "Those Beatitudes are something, aren't they?"

That same skepticism greeted my wife, Susan, when she stopped at a Catholic bookstore to pick up a Bible she'd ordered for me. The conversation with the clerk went something like this:

Clerk: "Confirmation present?"

Susan: "Nope. Birthday present for my husband."

Clerk *(with a look of surprise on her face):* "Does he *want* it?"

Now, if I managed that store I'd give the clerks a lesson in sales tactics. Their job is to *sell* Bibles, not voice incredulity when somebody tries to buy one.

But this clerk apparently was amazed that men would be interested in reading the Bible — much less studying it, even though interest in such study has been blossoming in recent years. After all, reading the Bible gets dangerously close to spiritual concerns, and spiritual concerns aren't macho. (On the other hand, a man jogging down the street at some ridiculously early hour, sporting an earphoned radio, and wearing skintight, shiny shorts raises nary an eyebrow.) Who says women should have a corner on spiritual matters?

Fortunately for our men's group, we got the chance to redeem ourselves. After another renewal weekend we began to attend real live, honest-to-goodness Bible studies. We opted to start on a more basic level. We wanted to get to know one another better, supporting when necessary and congratulating when appropriate. But most of all we wanted to be able to challenge one another to grow in faith.

And we did all this by adhering to an outline aimed at developing our Christian witness and community contributions. Each week we asked one another how we had experienced Christ during the past seven days — be it through people, what we'd read, something we'd seen, or an expression we'd heard. We had the freedom to speak up or remain silent, but the overriding aim and frequent result was that we eagerly began to look for Christ in our everyday lives. Our purpose was to make Christ happen, as we closed each meeting with a statement of at least one thing we planned to do the next week. Sometimes we followed through; other times we had to admit sheepishly that we'd coasted through the week.

Gradually we began experiencing Christ more, in ourselves and in one another, as well as in those we encountered elsewhere. Although we repeatedly vowed to get tougher with one another, to challenge ourselves to follow through more consistently and more meaningfully, we never quite reached that point. We might have, if relocations and different assignments hadn't fractured the group somewhat. But even without that, there was a marked improvement over our first shallow approach to Bible study. We grew together and separately, and some members of the group still meet, continuing the growth. But, most importantly, we developed a bond that persists in spite of distance or differing directions or varying intensities of our faith journeys.

Christ doesn't intend for us to make our journeys alone. As Father John Powell wrote in his *Unconditional Love,* quoting Charles Peguy: "Do not try to go to God alone. If you do, he will certainly ask you the embarrassing question: 'Where are your brothers and sisters?' "

If we do try it alone, we're no better than the "stupid" Galatians.

Thank You, Mr. Duggan and Uncle Frank

Mr. Mike Duggan was one of those neighbors who often was more like family than family.

The relationship started years ago when my son, Brendan, was only a tot. He thought Mr. Duggan was just a lad as well, despite their size difference and Mr. Duggan's pipe. In fact, Brendan usually referred to Mr. Duggan's wife, Opal, as Mr. Duggan's mom.

"Where's your mom?" he'd ask Mr. Duggan as he bedeviled our neighbor's car-tinkering, garden-puttering, and furniture-fixing endeavors. Brendan's developing mind simply figured that every guy had a mom in the house just like he did.

When Opal was outside and Mr. Duggan was nowhere to be seen, Brendan would approach her with the query, "Can Mr. Duggan come out and play?"

Brendan eventually determined that Mike and Opal were married, but the "Mr. Duggan" moniker persisted, making "I'm going over to Mr. Duggan's" one of the most common phrases around our house. Our youngest, Allison, picked up the habit when she came along, as well as Brendan's manipulative tricks in conning the Duggans out of candy. We warned both Allison and Brendan not to beg. But they'd stand in the Duggans' kitchen with one eye forlornly staring at the candy jar atop the refrigerator. Mike and Opal good-naturedly made the two underprivileged urchins play out their starving role before they'd suggest that the kids might want a piece of candy.

"Honest, Dad, I didn't ask," one or the other would vow when we went to the Duggans to get them. All the while, Mr. Duggan would wink knowingly in the background.

The Duggans always extended a helping hand when our young family got in a jam, whether it was pitching in on a fix-up project or donating plants to our feeble gardening attempts or just being there if we weren't home and the kids happened to lock themselves out of the house. Mr. Duggan was soft-spoken, always passing up the chance to say "I told you so" when we ignored his advice on the type of paint to buy or how to square a deck project or how to start a balky car. He'd just shake his head a little and proceed to show us how he had told us to do it in the first place.

Mr. Duggan and Opal wouldn't accept money, even when they did the lion's share of the work on a particular project. Oh, we did manage to get them to accept a couple of steaks after Mike helped us install a drop ceiling. But most of the time they simply replied, "That's what neighbors are for" when we offered our thanks.

Then Mr. Duggan got sick and we all felt sad. But our spirits rose when it looked like he was getting better. After all, he'd rebounded from the open-heart surgery a few years before, hadn't he? It seemed like a simple fact of life that Mr. Duggan was always going to be there, just like he always had been. Oh, we talked about the possibility that he might die, but we didn't really believe it.

I remember the day I skipped going over to chat with him, figuring I'd do it another time. But there wasn't another time. Mr. Duggan died.

I was quite concerned about how the kids would take his death. Annie, our eldest (fourteen), and Brendan (ten) had experienced the grief of death before, so it was not totally foreign to them. But it was a new sorrow for six-year-old Allison. She seemed hesitant to talk about it. She resisted going to the casket to see her pal for the last time.

But she insisted on laboriously signing her name in the visitors' book. She took the pen, ran across the room, and grabbed a tissue. However, she didn't use it to wipe away her tears. Instead, she painstakingly drew a tear-dripping heart with an arrow through it. That was her way to express the grief that she couldn't find the words to voice.

I'd been afraid Allison would keep her grief bottled up. Instead, her childlike instincts gave her a healthy — and an incredibly touching — way to acknowledge the fact that death is a part of life. She knew how to say good-bye to her friend.

Allison's inability to express her grief verbally came to mind a few months later when my Uncle Frank died. I noticed many mourners grappling with the typical tongue-tied words of sympathy at the wake. It's a common human phenomenon that people still often freeze up when it's time to offer their condolences — despite numerous books about attitudes toward death and dying.

Often people hug each other while mumbling words of sympathy, but usually they are awkward about it and involuntarily try to avoid the eyes of the survivors. Their signs of uneasiness do little to salve the hurt.

But it was different at Uncle Frank's funeral. Frowns turned to smiles, then broad grins and, in some cases, unrestrained laughter. This change took place during the eulogy which I had volunteered to give. I found memories of him emerging from my subconscious as I drove to the funeral; many of these thoughts I'd never before reflected upon.

As I recalled our fishing trips together, his particular fondness for children, and the fact that he always had plenty of time for other people, it occurred to me that he had been Christ to us in all those activities. I mentioned during the eulogy, which actually was a recounting of several anecdotes about what Frank had done for me and others — that he would have been embarrassed to be described as a vehicle for Christ, an instrument of Christ's presence on earth. But that seemed to be the best way to describe the fact that he gave of himself so generously, without ever asking for anything in return.

That giving helped everyone who knew Frank become a little more whole on the journey toward his or her hoped-for wholeness with God after death. The concept of wholeness was particularly fitting in Frank's case because he suffered extremely from emphysema. Realizing that Frank deserved that wholeness of the afterlife made it easier for us to let him go, knowing that part of him would be with us through Christ.

I could have left those stories untold and just been part of a grieving family as friends and acquaintances grappled with their own uneasiness about death. But I discovered that sharing them like that not only brought the smiles — and a few tears — to the faces of family and friends but also prompted many of those present to swap more "Frank" stories that day. "Remember the time Frank did this....Remember the time Frank did that....Remember how Frank always used to..." began many a sentence that day.

Oddly enough, I'd never really thought of Frank that way — as an instrument of Christ — until I forced myself to reflect on the man and what he'd done. I wish I had, when he was alive, and I wish I'd have been able to tell him in so many words that I'd been talking to Christ without knowing it.

The funerals of Mr. Duggan and Uncle Frank left me much more aware of Christ walking in the shoes of and speaking through the mouths of many more people in my daily life, whether they are family members, coworkers, friends, or total strangers. The challenge to me now is to acknowledge the Christ who lives in them, rejoice in it, and proclaim it while they, too, are still alive.

I Chased My Son and Caught Myself

One evening I spent quite some time chasing my son all over the neighborhood but ended up catching myself instead.

I'll spare you the tawdry details of what prompted the chase, because they were so insignificant I can't even remember them myself. Suffice it to say that he shot out of the house like, well, like the house was on fire.

I was torn about what to do. My wife, Susan, was at work. I was supposed to be at a meeting in half an hour, and I didn't want to be late. But I also didn't want to leave home when World War III had just broken out. I determined to make an attempt before I left; otherwise my mind would be distracted throughout the meeting. Besides, it was going to be dark soon, and I wanted to make sure Brendan was home safely.

I was wearing a suit, and I didn't want to get it sweaty; but I figured all I'd have to do was walk outside and find him in the backyard or, perhaps, in the garage. Wrong. However, I spied him down the alley a full block away about the same time he saw me looking for him. Even at that distance I could see he was frightened. I started walking after him — slowly, so I wouldn't get my suit sweaty. A pang of guilt pierced my chest that I'd scared him so much that he figured I was bent on bodily harm. (After all, physical punishment is rare around our house and he's reached a size where I've lost the little advantage I had anyway.)

My pace quickened when I reached the end of the alley and looked right, then left, without even catching a glimpse of him. I then realized that the suit was going to get sweaty anyway, so I started darting into yards, looking under porches, behind trees, and through bushes, all to no avail. I was getting impatient, but I'd already decided that I wasn't going to lose my temper when I did find him. It troubled me that he was so petrified. I wanted to have a nice, reasonable talk to determine why. And I wanted to apologize for frightening him so.

As my feet wandered, so did my mind; and I caught myself reflecting on the image of God I'd had as a child: a huge, bearded old man, with a booming voice, and an unforgiving mien — the type of person who easily could instill, well, the fear of the Lord in anyone. He was all-knowing and all-seeing, especially when a person stepped out of line. Adam and Eve cowering in a corner of the Garden was a popular portrayal. "God'll get you for that" was a common expression in those days.

Of course, my images have changed. God is a friendlier sort now — kind, gentle, forgiving. But that old image lingers, and sometimes I forget God's forgiving side. I run and hide when I've done something wrong or go to him only when I want something. In a way, I'm still like a child who has misbehaved.

It was this thought that brought my mind back to the task at hand: finding Brendan. So, after circling a couple more blocks, cutting through a few more alleys, and squeezing through several hedges, I finally gave up, figuring I'd just go home and wait. Imagine my surprise when I opened the kitchen closet door and saw Brendan floundering in the wastebasket. The prodigal son had beaten me home, squeezed into the closet to hide, fallen into the wastebasket, and now was stuck there like a cork in a bottle. His forlorn look broke any lingering tension on my part, and my smile apparently eased his fear.

By then I'd obviously given up on making it to the meeting on time. Brendan and I talked it over, and it appears that the volume and tone of my voice simply had scared him into thinking I was going to belt him one. But he discovered that I'm not really such a big ogre. And I was reminded (again) to control my temper.

The fact that in chasing Brendan, I actually caught myself reminded me that God the Father isn't really a mean, old man but rather a down-to-earth, warm, friendly, forgiving, and loving Father who sent his Son to redeem the world and left the Spirit here to guide it.

These qualities of warmth, friendliness, forgiveness, and love are evidenced in the way one person treats another. I chased my son and caught myself. He forgave me and I forgave him.

Spending More Time With the Family

The ladder kept me up most of the time, but I felt a letdown that evening. The good part was that being atop the ladder put me closer to heaven that day — assuming, of course, that heaven is up. But the precarious perch also separated me from my family, and that was the bad part of it.

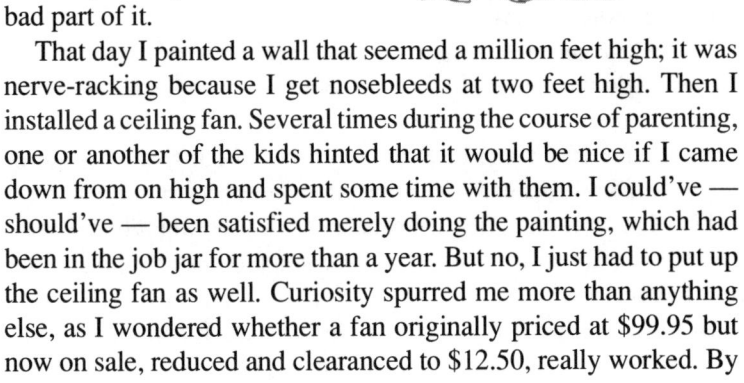

That day I painted a wall that seemed a million feet high; it was nerve-racking because I get nosebleeds at two feet high. Then I installed a ceiling fan. Several times during the course of parenting, one or another of the kids hinted that it would be nice if I came down from on high and spent some time with them. I could've — should've — been satisfied merely doing the painting, which had been in the job jar for more than a year. But no, I just had to put up the ceiling fan as well. Curiosity spurred me more than anything else, as I wondered whether a fan originally priced at $99.95 but now on sale, reduced and clearanced to $12.50, really worked. By

53

George, it did! I stood there, mildly surprised, admiring the spinning blades and patting myself on the back when a haunting voice from an invisible source started badgering me.

"So what?" the voice taunted.

"Huh?" I responded.

"So you think the fan's neat, and it was a great bargain, and you're pleased as punch with yourself that it works. But so what?"

"Well…" I started to respond to this nagging, overly conscientious conscience.

Then, rudely, interrupting, "It may keep spinning long after you're dead and gone, but it's just a cheap fan whose blades won't even stir a breeze in the wider scope of eternity. And who's going to know you put it up? Or care?"

That kind of badgering sure knocked the wind out of my sails, not to mention the air out of the fan. In fact, I even began to wish I hadn't bought it. I became a little depressed, contemplating the futility of jousting at ceiling fans and echoes in my head.

But then I finally figured out the message. I'd been preoccupied with *things* that day. I'd totally misplaced my priorities, opting for household chores I actually detested — especially painting high walls and ceilings — instead of spending time with my family. I'd chosen inanimate objects over flesh and blood, and meaningless tasks over potential growth opportunities.

I also cheated Susan and the kids out of a memory. If I'd suggested doing something — even something simple, like a board game or a game of pitch and catch or whatever — my family and I might have had something to remember about that afternoon. Years from now, instead of reminiscing about how much fun they had on that weekend, they'll probably be wondering where I was that day, recalling only that I often seemed too busy to spend time with them.

Unfortunately, the revelation didn't solidify for me until long after everybody else was in bed. Of course, I felt inclined to shake everybody awake, hug them, and tell them I love them. But that idea seemed foolish. They probably wouldn't even remember it the next day. Besides, if I hadn't had the courtesy to acknowledge their presence during the day, what right did I have rousing them from a sound sleep?

For some time after that I practiced the lesson I had learned so well. On several nights and even several weekends, I deliberately set aside some time with everybody in the family. I'll not even bother to discuss whether it was "quality time," because that's become such a cliché. I had to start slowly with a stress on at least *some* time.

But then I lapsed into feeling pressed to get "things" accomplished again. I started saying "not now, maybe later" or "we'll talk about it some other time." I guess I'll struggle throughout my life reminding myself that consistent, day-to-day time with family members is just as important, perhaps more, than a few camping trips and fishing expeditions.

In one of her columns Dolores Curran tweaked my conscience about that struggle. She wrote about a father and son who went on a fishing expedition but returned without any fish. When they got home, each entered a passage about the day in his own personal journal. The father recorded the fact that the fish weren't biting, so it was pretty much a waste of time. The son wrote in glowing phrases about how much fun it had been to go fishing with his dad on such a nice day.

What differing perspectives! I read the story over and over, each time feeling a new twinge of regret that I too often think I have to be "doing" something to prove that I'm alive. I should write a slogan on my bathroom mirror reminding me each day to spend time — yes, even just "waste" time — with every family member, and perhaps at least one other person outside the family.

The odd part about the struggle is that my work at a Catholic newspaper brings stories about discipleship and evangelism across my desk almost daily. But I — like far too many others, I'm afraid — still miss the point that acting on those two concepts doesn't have to involve large groups in grandiose settings. On the contrary, they should start right in the home, where Christ is present in each and every member of the family.

Discipleship and evangelism begin at home, where charity also begins, because they spring so naturally from charity. What good does it do to preach Christ to strangers if I don't have the faith to live it at home? That's the top rung on the ladder of hypocrisy!

I'm learning to come down from the ladder now and spend more time with my family.

Let Go and Let Drive

I hadn't even adjusted psychologically to the fact that the oldest in the family, Annie, had earned her driver's license when she asked that dreaded question: "Dad, can I have the car tomorrow night?"

The traumatic tumblings of my mind increased considerably as the question echoed in my ears. I tried to analyze why her request affected me so strongly. After all, she'd exhibited a lot of potential during her training forays, although she retained her penchant for checking both ways only when she was well into the middle of an intersection. And she cornered much too fast for my comfort.

Why, then, was I so troubled? Could it be

• That I recalled the first time I ever got to use the family car and a fire hydrant leaped in front of me and crushed the radiator, a block from home? I not only had two friends in the car who were not on my parents' officially endorsed "allowed passenger list" but also left my sister at the pizza place instead of bringing her home. More than the radiator hit the fan that night.

57

But I decided that experience wasn't the cause of my concern about Annie's driving. Why, an accident under such circumstances could happen to anybody, especially since fire hydrants are so lax in looking both ways.

- That I remember the first time I ever used our family's dry-cleaning van for a night out and ended up chasing a carload of girls on a back road in Nebraska — with my headlights off because I didn't want the pursuing police car to see me make my turn? And how nervous I was the next day every time I drove the van from my deliveries back to the dry-cleaning shop, afraid that a police car would be there?

No, I figured, that couldn't be it either. Annie is much too intelligent to try to outrun police. Besides, she was in a car and not a van with our name emblazoned across it. And back roads are fewer and farther between these days.

- That I recollected the first night I used the very first car of my own — a tired old '63 Volkswagen — on the highway, and a state patrol officer pulled me over for speeding? But the officer was sympathetic and believed my story that the reason I went downhill so fast was to get up enough speed to make it up the next hill.

No, I thought, that couldn't be the problem. I'd told Annie to drive slowly, and there's no way she'll be able to afford a mortgage on a car until she's at least forty.

A headache sneaked up on me. It intensified and wouldn't let go for a full day as I pondered what could be so upsetting about the fact that my daughter now had a driver's license. I knew that I would have to quit putting off the answer to her question about having the car the next night.

The solution came like a flash, unwelcome and jolting. My wife, Susan, called me at work with this blunt, brutal statement: "Mike, you don't have to pick up Annie at work. She drove herself." I was stunned, then hurt — confronted with the reality that I felt like my daughter didn't need me anymore. I, who had complained for years about how *my* schedule was interrupted constantly to bus children hither and yon and back again, suddenly was pouting because I didn't have to do it anymore. I who had longed for such relief now was in a tailspin of feeling sorry for myself. I felt expendable. Like a spare tire, it seemed I was needed only in an emergency, if then.

The very thought of this concrete sign that I might be losing Annie to her own independence thrust me into a reverie about why I felt possessive in the first place. After all, I'd always known intellectually that God just loans children to parents, and it's just for a little while. But I hadn't expected the recall to be so soon. I had figured it might come when she went to college or got her own apartment or got married.

But not so soon. Not now. Not like this.

I looked at the other two kids that night, wondering when the same thing would happen with them. Would it be under the same circumstances or different ones? Was I overreacting or would this continue a pell-mell move toward separation? But most of all, I wondered why I was finding it so hard to let go, in such a little way, even after I realized that I *was* overreacting. Why did I fail to recognize that I was entering a period of growth rather than separation?

The more I thought, the more I realized that I was perhaps afraid I haven't quite lived up to God's expectations with the kids, that too often I've been too busy, that I've not done enough with them. And, as I noticed how often the word "I" was cropping up in my thoughts, it finally dawned on me that I wasn't supposed to be the controller anyway.

After all, God is the ultimate controller. He turns persons loose in the world with a free will, letting each one choose whether to follow Christian values or ignore them. What right do I have to control the kids then? At this point all I can do is hope that I've succeeded in instilling basic values and letting the kids decide to live their own lives.

Annie's question reminded me of the advice, "Let go and let God." In this case it was "let drive," and Annie got to use the car.

As I feigned sleep while waiting for her to come home that first night — pretending I wasn't worried about whether she'd eventually arrive — I realized that there's still time for growth together, and separately. Hopefully, it will be with God.

Recalling the God of the Past

Bad Old Days — or Good Old Days?

There is reason to suspect that the "bad old days" were not nearly as bad as the stories that people use to revile them, any more than the "good old days" were actually as good as the fond memories that people revel in.

Horror stories abound about the scars people allegedly retain from Catholic education methods of the past. Often these stories take a humorous tack, with the proliferation of books, jokes, plays, and movies about irascible old monsignors and crabby, ruler-wielding nuns — or, as they were sometimes called, 'Sters. Granted, some of these stories are grounded in fact, and it is hoped that the people involved will eventually be healed. But hyperbole also plays a role, as exaggeration helps make an average anecdote a good one, and a good one a great one, when people compare notes about their upbringing. Most Catholics learned a lot of good, basic values that heavily influence their lives today, and they shouldn't let that good get lost in their enthusiasm to accent the negative for effect.

These thoughts occurred to me after a visit with my eighth-grade teacher, whom I'd admired and nearly idolized as one of my favorites while she was principal for most of my grade-school years. I hadn't heard from Dominican Sister Marie Loyola — or she from me — for roughly a quarter century until the time she called me at work one day. Our paths had split after my eighth-grade graduation, which also happened to be the time she was assigned to go elsewhere.

Her phone call stirred memories of smiles — both mine and the ones I remember crossing her face often — of her brisk walk down the halls, robes flowing behind her, of wondering how she could survive on a measly orange for lunch and, yes, of speculating about the color of the hair beneath her veil.

(Of course, I also can recall a few frowns, as her glare could melt ice in Antarctica if anyone were dumb enough to cross her. I vividly remember one April Fools' Day when I did so. I pinned a "kick me" sign on the back of the fourth-grade teacher. Bomb shelters were the "in" thing those days and, suffice it to say without going into the gory details, I sure wish I could've hidden in one for the rest of the day to avoid the tongue-lashing I got. But Sister wasn't one to hold grudges for long, and she and I were friends once the dust had cleared.)

After that phone call, she and I were able to get together for a short visit before she left town. Our reminiscences were delightful. Sister said she couldn't recall the April Fools' Day incident, but she seemed to remember the name and family background of almost every student I mentioned.

However, a few of her comments started to bother me. "Back then," she noted, "I taught what I was told to teach." She also observed that, if she had it to do over, she'd take more time to talk to the students, smile more, and not scream as much. (It always amazed me how she could juggle her duties of secretary, janitor, and teacher of forty-five students in one class.)

63

I wondered what prompted her to voice those thoughts. Was it just my imagination or was she making an apology? Without mentioning that wonderment, I told her I have tons of great memories about her and about Catholic schools in general, and I know others who do too. Like all Catholics, I feel indebted to Sisters like her and others who laid my educational foundations, even though I sometimes joke about the foundation stones.

At the end of our visit, I told her I love her, and she said the same about me. We hugged and parted. I haven't seen her since, although we've corresponded a few times since then.

But it dawned on me then, and I try to be sensitive to it now, that whatever has been said and done — the jokes, the innuendos in books and movies — probably have hurt a lot of these Sisters. This is especially true when the criticism is excessive and isn't accompanied by any positive strokes at all. Those Sisters, Brothers, and priests served the Church quite well. Many, like Sister Marie Loyola, served in the days of huge class sizes and no breaks and through the turmoil of change. And they continue to serve today, often beyond retirement age.

Unfortunately, people haven't differentiated between jokes aimed at institutions and darts that inadvertently pierce the hearts of others. I hope those servants who brought Christ to so many Catholics when they were younger don't feel like they've been wronged. If they do feel so, there is need for apology.

I'm glad my visit with Sister Marie Loyola sensitized me about how much those people meant — and still mean — to me. Oh, I still tell the jokes and laugh at the books, as it seems to be a part of the heritage. But I also try to keep everything in context, and I'll try to keep in better contact with Sister and others who have helped me on my journey over the years. The list is long, and I've got some catching up to do.

But the "good old days" far outweighed "the bad ones," and it'll be worth the effort at renewing contacts.

Lent Yesterday and Lent Today

"**H**ave you ever ransomed a pagan baby?"

That question may sound strange to modern youth, but the practice of "ransoming" pagan babies was a key element of the Lenten season in the parochial school I attended, as it was in most Catholic schools of those days.

Even though the ransoming was such a big part of the season, I totally forgot about it until one evening when the question of what happened to all those pagan babies just popped into my head. As I recall, the ransoming process became almost a contest. The classes pooled their pennies, nickels, and dimes to reach the goal of $5 to ransom a baby from paganism in a far-off land. Of course, many boys and girls were so enthusiastic that they tried to ransom the babies single-handedly. In fact, I personally saved several, each of whom I dutifully named and prayed for.

There is no reason, however, to applaud my apparent acts of largess because even my parents didn't know I was becoming a ransom lord until one of the nuns told them what a great, self-sacrificing and generous person I was. The news surprised my parents, from whom I'd been pilfering the money. And, also as I recall, they passed the surprise right along to the area of my anatomy where I store my billfold, now that I have money of my own.

This recollection led me to conclude that the pagan baby ritual of my youth actually was flawed. The message of what I was supposed to be doing often didn't sink in. Like the others, I became so engrossed in the process of raising more and more money, and one-upmanship, that I missed the point that those were real live human beings on the receiving end. (And no doubt I wasn't the only one who resorted to petty thievery, totally negating any possible positive impact.)

Quite likely the contributions helped, and many of those "pagan babies" are probably living active Catholics today. Maybe thanks to me, maybe not. Certainly, I deserve little thanks in most cases for ransoming so many and remembering so few.

At any rate my nostalgia prompted me to ask our oldest, Annie, whether she and her classmates were ransoming babies. To my delight, she responded with the stare of disdain that often crosses her face when she thinks I'm going daft, saying, "Whuddya mean, pagan babies?"

I explained the process briefly, as her expression changed to its "omigosh-I-trapped-myself-into-another-good-old-days-story" look. Sometimes she feigns politeness; more often she displays impatience. She was appearing more and more impatient with my tales of saving pagans in far-flung, impoverished areas of the globe. So I shortened the story and asked what she was doing for Lent these days.

I was happy to discover that the emphasis is on positive, thought-provoking actions instead of the age-old "giving up" popcorn, candy, or movies. I like the positive approach; it encourages acts of kindness, justice, and overall charity. After all such actions certainly incorporate the gospel message into the lives of all. And they often even extend beyond Lent — so unlike my buy-them-and-drop-them plan of ransoming babies.

Other activities — Operation Rice Bowl, for example — combine sacrifice with a learning experience. They give people a certain empathy with the disadvantaged, as they actually try to put themselves in their shoes, if they have any. Other programs encourage prayer, fasting, and almsgiving. Some money stays in local dioceses to help relieve hunger there as well. What's more, such programs also aim to provide the disadvantaged with tools and training to help themselves.

In short, such activities are not handouts, but hands out helping — supporting hands of enlightened social action. Who knows? Perhaps these present-day development efforts are helping those babies ransomed by the Catholic youth of decades past.

I Was Afraid I'd Lose My Soul to a Chocolate Malt

Thanks to an incredible amount of naiveté, I spent most of what could have been my summer to emerge from puberty carefully avoiding the proximate occasion of sin — chocolate malts.

On the last day of school each year, the principal gave a lengthy lecture warning her students not to lose their souls for a few moments of pleasure. I was so naive in the early days of high school that I honestly thought she was talking about something as "dangerous" as reveling in a chocolate malt. I'm not exaggerating to make a point or using poetic license to entertain. In fact, it's rather embarrassing to have to admit that I knew so little about the facts of life that I didn't even know she was talking about sex. I believed she was talking about anything that might lead to an undue amount of pleasure. (And I found chocolate malts the way they used to make them to be very, very pleasing.) Of course, actually talking about sex as sex in those days was almost taboo. I knew generally that the priests and nuns wanted boys and girls to fraternize as little as possible. But they spoke of it so euphemistically, and I was so dense, that I wasn't sure why.

The idea of foregoing the cool richness of malts to escape the fires of hell threw me into a quandary of another sort. I was little more than skin and bones in high school, and I'd planned to drink a malt a day that summer to bulk myself up for basketball. (Oh, to have that metabolism back instead of having to struggle with middle-aged spread now!) But Sister's admonition echoed in my ears whenever I lingered longingly outside an ice-cream parlor, as it was called in those days.

"Don't lose your soul for a few moments of pleasure, Michael," I could almost hear her words, as if she'd been addressing her warnings only to me.

So I spent the summer golfing with my dad and carefully avoiding ice-cream parlors. I've nothing against my Dad or golfing because those are some of the fondest memories of my youth (until he started winning). Meanwhile many of my friends who actually knew what Sister had been talking about not only were drinking malts but also were drinking them with girls — and out of the same glass, for all I knew. They returned to school a little heavier and a lot wiser in the ways of the world, while I was still skinny and getting shoved around on the basketball court.

There was always another reminder of this when basketball playoffs started rolling around; even those who didn't pay attention to the team during the regular season got the message. The tipoff was when the superintendent called an assembly in the gym, with the boys on one side and girls on the other, naturally. Father would mention that spring was coming, and that's the time when young people would get a little rambunctious. Boys might start noticing girls a little more, he'd say, and vice versa. But that should not be, he'd warn, if the team wanted to make it to the state playoffs.

Then he'd turn his attention specifically to the girls, imploring them not to distract the boys from this grand endeavor. (Only years later, after male-female sensitivities had risen, did it dawn on me that his lectures always placed the burden of actions or inaction on the girls. He didn't tell the boys to leave the girls alone. Instead he admonished the girls to leave the boys alone so they wouldn't be distracted. But the obvious bias here is an entirely different issue that would make a book unto itself, so I'll merely leave it at that.)

Every year the team entered the basketball playoffs with few distractions, but never made it to state.

While it seems humorous now to recall these efforts to control teenage libidos, there's also a sad side to it. The problem was that I was being told what *not* to do all the time, but I don't recall being told what I *should* do to develop healthy boy-girl relationships. I remember a priest telling the class that a prolonged hug would be a mortal sin, because that would indicate ownership and young people had no rights in this area. I left the room asking myself how long a prolonged hug was. Was it ten, thirty, fifty seconds, a full minute? The priest left me hanging and hung up with an ambiguous and questionable guideline about something I shouldn't do. But what should I do in the meantime?

Fortunately, the manner of teaching morality has changed. And, even though teens today are more pressured than when I was young, at least churches, schools and, in some cases, parents are trying to equip them with more information about how to cope. Whether they listen is debatable from day to day, but that's part of the human condition. The pressures of complicated relationship, too much mobility and money, drugs, and — yes — sex weigh heavily on teenagers. And those pressures, in part, have helped force the adult world to be more up-front about what they *shouldn't* do and begin to stress more what they *should* do.

I disagree somewhat with the "just say no" effort on drugs because that reminds me of what I had to do to those malts beckoning me to gulp. Besides, young people can see through that and ask for reasons why. If they are not provided alternatives — so they don't feel attracted to drugs — the slogan will fall on deaf ears. In much the same way, my maltless summer didn't help me in the area of sex because I wasn't even aware that was the issue. What a void that left, as far as helping me figure out what to do positively.

Today teenagers — and adults, for that matter — also learn that sex outside of marriage is wrong, but they learn the right reasons. Now people are taught that sex is a gift from God, one that is so precious that it is to be reserved for marriage. In addition, choosing not to have extramarital sex actually is a better way of showing love than exercising the biological function. It proves to others that they are truly liked and loved. All people are gifts of God, and they must not be robbed of their gift of sex.

Instead of being told that a prolonged hug is a mortal sin, people today are told that hugs can be wholesome ways of showing affection, friendship, concern. The positive approach of ascribing values — human and God-given — contributes to positive results. Instead of closing their eyes, they're opening them and — hopefully — helping to open the eyes of those for whom they are responsible.

Meeting God Through Random Reflections

Is There Life After Hockey?

The winter wind that tossed the tassel on my stocking cap, driving the wind chill of the ten-degree temperature down to a minus twenty-three and frosting my mustache, also blew the above question into my red-tipped ears as I watched my son, Brendan, and his teammates try to score on that moonlight night. The message was as clear as the clouds of breath hanging in front of my face, haunting me as the tips of my fingers lost their feeling and my feet became numb.

People often wonder whether there is life after death. But do they consistently put as much time and effort into preparing for the afterlife as they do for pursuits such as sports or other forms of entertainment? Arguments abound that entirely too much money, time, and attention are spent on sports of all sorts.

What some people do when they have a child in a hockey program — or any other sports program, for that matter — provides evidence of how skewed priorities can become. They're either putting on or taking off kids' expensive hockey skates for practice or games. (And this while hundreds — thousands, or even hundreds of thousands — have trouble finding adequate shelter.)

I've seen and heard coaches — and, sadly, sometimes, parents — berate youngsters for slipping up on the ice. (And this, too, while countless elderly, orphans, or just plain lonely people yearn for an encouraging, kind word but face the painful reality that another day will pass with no visitors, no letters, no gentle touch.)

People fret about the most recent injury to a professional athlete — not necessarily because they're concerned about the health of the person, but because they're worried about wins, losses, and — maybe — their bets. (And this while the children of a broken home go without adequate medical care for lack of insurance.)

Of course, sports aren't the only place where people invest their time and money in questionable priorities. They plunk down twenty dollars, thirty dollars, or even forty dollars for a concert or dance or dinner without even thinking about it or wondering whether it's really worth that much money. (And this again while charity workers struggle to mend a few broken toys to brighten the eyes of poor youngsters for a holiday.)

These thoughts spun in my mind that night, even as the wind continued to freeze my face and wisps of blown snow prompted me to blink involuntarily. I recalled the days a couple weeks before when I almost opted to forgo Mass because it looked too cold to venture out. But there I stood that night, shivering and stomping my feet, watching hockey. It wasn't too cold for hockey.

I guiltily remembered the recent Sunday morning when the requirements of hockey scheduling led to such a hectic time that Church ended up getting iced. My kid's supposed to be learning from me, I thought, but do I spend as much time showing him the joys of God's love, of the Spirit's work, of Christ's supreme loving act as I do carting him to hockey practice, making sure his skates are sharp, cheering at the games, or locker-room talking before and after games? Do I take the time to work with him, gathering items for a food shelf, serving a meal at a shelter, dropping by a nursing home? Do I talk just blue lines and red lines, or do I take the time to point out that many in this world are forced to live from food line to food line, that something should be done about that?

The answer was as clear as the crisp night air. Too often, Church, spirituality, and social justice end up in the penalty box, or I end up offside. I realized that I'd better start preparing better for life after hockey. And that includes not only working on my own spiritual life but also working to improve the temporal and spiritual lives of others — starting with an awareness at home that spreads into community action.

Warning: Bumps Ahead

There seems to be no rhyme or reason for the placement of the "bump" signs on highways. After all, they provide scant warning, appearing out of nowhere about six yards before the bump, followed shortly by another sign with a big arrow pointing exactly at the bump.

When this happens to us our heads poke a dent in the roof, the kids bounce all over the car or reel from the recoil of their seat belts, and our shock absorbers shudder ominously.

Life also offers sundry bumps — some forewarned, others not — and we have to have faith in God, ourselves, and our fellow human beings that we'll land on our wheels. Oh, a tire may go flat once in a while, but that's a surmountable problem. The main idea is to keep everything in perspective and remember that prayer and other people can help us get back on the journey.

We are told that God never gives us more problems than we can handle. That's a nice little saying, but it's often easier to say it than to live it. Indeed, it's often hard to even remember it when problems seem to loom ever larger at every turn in the road.

Faith is so flexible. One day when the sun is shining, the birds are chirping, and the car is working smoothly, it's easy to believe. Another day when the skies are gray and a gully-washer of a rainstorm floods the road and stalls the engine, it's hard to believe in anything, especially rainbows.

Our spouses can be a source of love and comfort, especially when everything's going well and there are smiles all around. But when conflicts arise or when we disagree on something so silly as who gets which section of the paper first, they can seem as irritating as a balky carburetor. Our children can be a source of delight when they're bubbling with enthusiasm and joy and not fighting. But when they get crabby or won't pick up their clothes, or we want to go out and can't find a sitter, they can seem as troublesome as a clogged gas line. Our jobs can be a source of satisfaction and growth when the computer is working and the boss gives us encouraging words. But when the computer is down and the boss is overly demanding and not so understanding, it can seem like we're trying to navigate life's bumps on four flats.

Yes, the drive through life offers its bumps and curves and sometimes potholes so big we could drive around in them for days before we find our way out. At times those bumps can signal the need to switch lanes or find an exit for a break from the routine. Those are the times for reflection and prayer, for checking the oil on our relationships with God, our families, our friends, and our coworkers. These people can be irritating, but it's good to remember that we're not always so pleasant ourselves. Besides they're the ones who can help smooth the road, straighten the curves, and cushion the bumps on our road of life.

Jousting at Dirt Hills

I am convinced that if I enter the afterlife of the damned instead of the saved my punishment will be to care for the largest, rockiest, hilliest yard imaginable on earth or, well, in hell. I despise dirt and loathe leaves.

Nonetheless, I have an inexplicable, but compulsive, habit of starting just a "little" yard project every summer. These projects are nothing flamboyant or even particularly inspired. In fact, they often amount to no more than moving "tons" of dirt from one side of the yard one summer, only to change my mind and move it back the next.

This idiosyncrasy has made me the butt of countless jokes. People I don't even know walk up to me on the street and ask where I'm moving the yard this year. I lie and tell them I've given up, knowing full well that the worn and slightly muddy knees of my jeans and one persistent blister on my shovel hand give me away. Meanwhile the pile of discarded dirt near the alley rises and falls as I move it here, there, and everywhere.

By some miraculous stroke a couple of these projects have turned out to be mildly presentable improvements. But most of them just confirm my family's fears and neighbors' allegations that I'm just an eccentric who has absolutely no idea what I'm doing when I pick up a yard or garden tool.

The truth is that I have no idea what compels me to start another project every spring. I'd much rather be fishing or golfing. But I find myself instead leaning wistfully on a shovel as golfers drive by and wave. I do know that I don't do it as a faith experience. Even so, I've found that stepping back and reflecting on the success or lack of same have shown me parallels between shoveling at dirt hills and jousting at what often seem to be the windmills of faith.

Take the patio project, as Susan so often wished somebody would. That one sure brought the "why-dontchas" over to our house. For those who haven't done yard work, the "why-dontchas" are neighbors who come over to watch you work. They feel obligated to supervise and criticize.

"Why-dontcha do it this way?" they'll ask. "Why-dontcha do it that way?"

The "why-dontchas" on that patio project nearly drove me crazy — saying this wouldn't work and that would fail. But I stuck to my plans and believe it or not, it worked. (Of course, now I've moved and the couple who bought the house apparently didn't agree. I understand they've built an addition over what used to be the patio. There's no accounting for taste or lack of same.)

The "why-dontchas" during my terracing project turned downright hostile. In fact, the common question became "why-didja?" I'd gotten several large slabs of marble, slate, and other stone and used them to shore up the dirt on a couple levels of terracing. The catcalls began immediately, as virtually everyone agreed that it looked like a graveyard. Several people wondered why there were no inscriptions on the "headstones." One vandal — actually, I suspect it was my mother-in-law — even wrote "RIP" on several of the stones. A neighbor sent her visiting daughters out to view the project, and they laughed so hard they nearly fell over each other. They thought I didn't see, but I saw. I have feelings. I was hurt.

The problem was, the nay-sayers looked at the terracing and saw nothing more than a bunch of propped-up stones. I closed my eyes and envisioned colorful flowers growing between the slabs and cascading over them. I closed my ears to the taunts and planted the seeds. To my delight and their surprise, the flowers did exactly as I'd prayed they would. The critics' laughter subsided, and I was more than pleased when they begrudgingly admitted that the project had turned out well.

Of course, I knew all along that the fall would bring a different story. The plants would die, allowing the ugly stones to rear their craggy edges again. And, indeed, that did happen, most inconveniently right before Halloween. A stranger to the neighborhood who obviously hadn't seen the beflowered terrace told me it was very nice of me to build something so eerie to scare the kids on October 31.

But for me the return of the barren faces of the stones provided another faith statement, just as the bare branches of trees do for so many every fall. Trees willingly give up their leaves to nature's cycle, having faith that spring will bring them buds and leaves to burst into greenery for another summer. And I knew that my stones, aided by careful planting and weeding and cultivating, would serve again as a backdrop to green leaves and colorful flowers.

I've had to face somewhat similar circumstances as described above in my own faith life. It has nothing to do with my feelings about yard work, because I'm definitely more open to working on my faith life than my yard — most of the time, anyway. No, it has to do with the numerous "why-dontchas" and "why-didjas" on my journey. These challenges, I have to admit, sometimes do contain suggestions that are very useful, and I'm thankful for that. But other ideas are only marginally helpful to me personally, and some are totally useless. Something that works fabulously to help one person develop his or her faith life may simply confuse another. The secret is taking the time to sort through the ideas, concepts, and techniques and determine what's right for the individual.

Unfortunately, we tend not to leave one another alone and try to impose our ideas on others. We forget that there can be several ways to experience Christ. We narrow our actions to our concept of the "only way" and expect others to acknowledge it.

Fortunately, we've become more tolerant of other faiths. But sadly, we often don't bring that lesson home to our fellow Catholics. Liberals and conservatives seem to look more for differences than for agreements and drive the divisive wedge in even farther. But happily, while some in the hierarchical and theological circles argue, a great many in the pews persist in developing their faith despite the hubbub.

Just as there's more than one way to terrace a yard — each with its own pluses and minuses, but each with its own potential for beautiful flowering — there is more than one way to develop a relationship with Christ. Participation in the Eucharistic celebration of the Mass is the perfect vehicle for some, while a walk in nature can have a similar effect for others; the rosary is the key for many, while spontaneous prayer unlocks the door for others; community service draws some closer to God, while private prayers of intercession fulfill others. Each method helps to build up the community.

But for each to succeed, we must become less critical of one another and more open to others' ideas. We all have our own weeds to uproot and barren stones to cherish, without playing the game of "why-dontcha" with others' faith life.

Finding Christ Everywhere

I always learn something new at the conventions I attend from time to time; and the three stories that follow are living proof of that. I heard them at a gathering of youth ministers.

The first story was told by a youth minister who confessed that she had repeatedly rejected a teenage girl's invitations to visit her farm. Acknowledging the sincerity of the girl's invitations, she simply couldn't bring herself to go to the farm. The very idea was disgusting to her. She shuddered at how udderly — uh, sorry — gross she had imagined a barnyard would be. Even though she is a native of a midsized Illinois city, she rarely had seen any farm animals.

Even though she felt bad about turning the girl down, she just did not want to sully her shoes and shock her senses in an Iowa farmyard. After all, farms are for farmers, and stores are for city folks. Farmers grow the food and raise the livestock, and city residents simply go to the store to pinch the produce, pluck the plastic-wrapped chickens from refrigerated shelves, and winnow through the boxed cereals to find the brand of bran that promotes health and regularity. Right?

As a city girl, she couldn't imagine how in the world a person could enjoy traipsing around a farm. She wondered why anyone would want to get up at five o'clock every day to milk cows.

The farm girl persisted in her invitations, and the youth minister finally ran out of excuses. She said okay, albeit begrudgingly.

However, much to the youth minister's surprise, the clay of her negative images was remolded as she watched the young farm girl do her chores. The girl sat silently on a bucket as she monitored the machines coaxing the milk from the cows. Spiritual music issued softly from speakers in the barn, and the girl closed her eyes occasionally.

The visitor's fear of the perils, the smells, and the drudgery of farm life disappeared in awe as she noticed how prayerful a time this was for her hostess. She marveled at how completely this teenager was able to shut out all worries of the world and visit with her God.

This story made me recall the peacefulness of the days when I lived on a farm with two other young bachelors: the serenity of the sun rising over the distant hills, playfully changing the shadows in the valley as it climbed into the sky to herald a new day; the startled look on the face of one roommate when he glanced up from supper and found himself staring into the countenance of an inquisitive cow peeking into our window; and the perfect quiet of a still moonlit night.

I was roused from my reflections when the youth minister continued her story, happily noting that she has returned to the farm several times since that first visit. She told of walking where she once feared to step and marveling at the spirituality she was so surprised to find there.

The others agreed with her discovery of a closeness to God, an appreciation for life, a wellspring of hope, that can be encountered on a farm. During troubled times people find comfort in returning to their rural roots. If they can't go back physically, they can at least close their eyes and imagine the sounds as well as the quiet, the odors as well as the aromas.

I awoke from these reveries when the youth minister posed the following question: "We know from this story that there is something that can be called *rural spirituality*, but is there something that can be called *urban spirituality?*"

The question caught her listeners off guard, and there followed an uneasy, embarrassed silence. I sensed the wheels of the others' minds turning, even as my own brain churned, groping for an intelligent answer. None came, so I wound down a notch and tried to think of any answer, intelligent or otherwise. Still, I drew a blank. Surely, there must be a spirituality of the city.

Fortunately, another youth minister supplied an answer to the question with the following story. She recalled a miserable, sleeting day during a holiday season in Chicago. People wrapped their coats tightly around themselves as they rushed from store to store doing their Christmas shopping. They barely missed a step as they bypassed a derelict huddled in a doorway, clutching a piece of cardboard around himself to ward off the icy rain.

A tear formed in her eye and her voice caught in her throat as she remembered with a sense of shame that she was one of those who had not stopped to help the man.

"He was Christ," she said simply.

Finally, a third youth minster told of visiting a Third World country while on a service project. One day he went with several others to a ramshackle house, a shack made of cardboard and other scraps. He recoiled when he saw the occupant, a man of grotesque appearance, whose body exuded a nearly unbearable stench.

As the others in the car got out and hugged the man, this youth minister realized that he too would be expected to embrace him. He hesitated in the car, afraid to step out but also afraid to hurt the man's feelings. He doubted whether he could hug the grotesque, foul-smelling man; but finally he walked slowly toward him and gingerly put his arms around him.

Suddenly a tremendous feeling of warmth coursed through his body. The filthy living conditions, the man's appearance, and the smell disappeared. He was overcome with a sense that he was embracing none other than Jesus Christ.

I have thought about these stories, and found myself haunted with the particular question about the spirituality of the city. What is it? Where is it? Is it different from that of the country?

When a friend said the word *spirituality* is a difficult one for her, something clicked. I realized that the word itself was getting in my way. My mind had become snarled in what amounted to a comparative spirituality, almost as if a rural spirituality might be "better" than an urban one, or vice versa. It finally occurred to me what a ridiculous pursuit that was.

I tried to set aside the word for a moment and look for a common denominator, and I felt stupid when I realized the answer was obvious. Instead of pinning down the precise meaning of a word, I discovered that God, Christ, was the common thread linking the three stories.

One youth minister found that it was possible in the midst of farm chores to converse with Christ. Another found Christ in a homeless man on a Chicago sidewalk. Still another found him in a poverty-stricken man in the Third World.

I'm still a tad puzzled about this secret of spirituality, but I have learned from the above stories that practical spirituality revolves around my relationship with God, with Christ, with the Holy Spirit.

Whether in a forest of trees or a tangle of traffic lights, God can be found everywhere. The important thing is that I look. That means that I must take the time to search for him in the people I encounter each day.

Empty Trays, Empty Lives

Empty ice-cube trays are one of the most consistently irritating frustrations of my life. That I have a pretty low boiling point my family agrees, readily and heartily.

Oh, my tantrums during countless demonstrations of how easy it is to refill the trays pay off periodically. Some family members usually manage to fill the trays occasionally for a few days after such outbursts. But my temper boiled like an overheated car radiator in the middle of the desert one sweltering evening when I opened the freezer and saw not one, not two, but two and a half empty trays.

A few angry thoughts rushed through my mind before my inner voice interrupted them: "Just cool down, Tighe. After all, that's kind of how your spiritual life has been lately."

"What do you mean?" I asked defensively.

"Don't be evasive and don't act so innocent," the voice scolded. "You've been pretty empty spiritually, just like those trays are empty. But what have *you* done to fill yourself up? How long's it been since you attended Mass on a weekday?"

"Well, uh…" I stammered, staring at the empty trays as if they were haunted.

"And haven't you been pretty frustrated lately?" the voice jabbed. "At work? At home? In between?"

Well, I had to admit, as I reluctantly refilled the trays, that the voice was right. There had been a few hassles at work. And family bickering seemed to be increasing rather than decreasing. Also I hadn't been taking the time to fish or golf or relax in general. The list could go on; suffice it to say that my life hadn't exactly been smooth sailing of late.

I usually try to attend daily Mass, a habit I picked up during the past five years or so of my spiritual journey. I do it for the same reasons many other people do it: It's great to start the day with the greatest prayer imaginable; it gives me a boost, making even a bad day seem better.

My family eventually started teasing me about my Mass attendance, labeling me "Marathon Mass Man." Their teasing intensified when I'd go on a Saturday morning and then Saturday evening as well for the Sunday observance. (I eventually realized my short-sightedness on weekends when I'd go twice on Saturday, but not on Sunday. I was misleading myself about attending Mass daily with that Saturday night loophole. After all, Sunday's a day too, the last time I checked.)

However, my daily attendance is sporadic; I'll go several days or even weeks in a row, and then miss several, for one reason or another. And I was in the middle of a cycle in which I'd missed several for a variety of reasons, some legitimate, but many others attributable only to a comfortable bed and a streak of laziness.

My inner voice forced me to look within myself, and I began to realize that my recent frustrated days coincided somewhat with my string of Massless days. I decided right then and there to be less concerned about matters I cannot change — like empty ice-cube trays — and focus instead on matters I can control — like going to Mass more often, for starters.

John 3:16 and Romans 10:9

At many sporting events in today's world we often see people holding up posters calling attention to certain Scripture quotations. Somebody with a placard citing John 3:16, for example, manages to edge into the TV picture. Recently, however, another poster has made the scene; it reads: "For, if you confess with your mouth that Jesus is Lord and believe in your heart that God raised him from the dead, you will be saved" (Romans 10:9).

Most of us are familiar with John 3:16: "For God so loved the world that he gave his only Son, so that everyone who believes in him might not perish but might have eternal life."

Of course, the interpretation affects the message received. Some might argue that John 3:16 and Romans 10:9 merely mean "believe and be saved." But it's quite possible that there's more to Romans 10:9. It seems to include the dimension of urging everyone to spread the faith. That rings true especially if 10:9 is read in context with the entire chapter, which refers to people being sent to preach. "How beautiful are the feet of those who bring [the] good news!" (Romans 10:15).

Unfortunately, Catholic feet haven't always been that good at spreading the news, other than missionaries' feet going to far-flung places. In the past many of us have hesitated about even walking across the street to evangelize. Maybe we figured we didn't know enough. Maybe we figured that belonging to the "one true faith" was sufficient. Or perhaps we weren't confident enough in our faith or in ourselves. We often restricted our outside-Mass activities to socials and suppers and festivals, but hesitated to get involved in something as threatening as education or — horror of horrors — spirituality.

But that has changed markedly in recent years with increased interest in spirituality, a new emphasis on Bible study, and even a penchant for evangelism. All of a sudden we're not only studying about our faith but also sharing it. We're finding that such endeavors not only strengthen our faith but make it more enjoyable at the same time.

So, after a little John 3:16 and a dose of Romans 10:9, maybe we're headed toward 1 Corinthians 9:16: "If I preach the gospel, this is no reason for me to boast, for an obligation has been imposed on me, and woe to me if I do not preach it!"

People sometimes criticize the TV placard-holders as pushy attention seekers. That seems a bit harsh and judgmental — which is not to suggest that everybody become walking billboards, any more than it suggests that run-of-the-mill athletes perform as all-stars.

To each his or her own, stylewise and timewise. A kind word, an encouraging sentence, a good example — or a poster on TV — can accomplish just as much as a scintillating sermon.

That One-more Syndrome...

We humans are so sensitive about so many maladies, both real and imagined, that we often forget about one of the most debilitating: the one-more syndrome. Unlike the serious and potentially fatal diseases such as AIDS, cancer, and heart disease that affect only a certain portion of us, the one-more syndrome infects us in the womb and follows us to the tomb.

Many of us foisted unreasonable amounts of time in labor upon our mothers as we tried to stay in the comfort and relative quiet of the womb for one more minute, one more hour, or one more day. From the point of birth on, hardly any of us escapes the disease of forever wanting *one more* this or *one more* that. No matter how much we have or how much we control or how happy we are, the one-more syndrome keeps us dissatisfied. Consider the following:

- The number of times we, as children, con our parents into lingering at the park for *one more* swing or *one more* slide or *one more* push on the merry-go-round. (Actually, it rarely ends up being only *one more* as the pleas for *one more* continue to tumble forth like water in a babbling brook.)
- How often we fall victim to *one more* helping at dinner or *one more* piece of candy as the proliferation of food and sweets settles collectively around the constantly broadening belly of a nation that is so overfed in so many instances yet starving in so many areas.
- Our pressing need to buy *one more* outfit, even though our closets are already bursting with almost-new clothing while thousands of homeless shiver helplessly underclothed in the cruel winter wind.
- Our habit of requesting — no, demanding — one more song, then another *one more* and another and another at a dance or a concert.
- The damage we inflict on our soil and water, hoping that *one more* bag of fertilizer or insecticide will bring in *one more* bushel of corn.
- The heartache caused daily from the persistent belief that *one more* for the road is just what we need.
- The danger we place ourselves in as we allow our governments to continue their quests for *one more* even more lethal and fail-safe missile to protect us from our rivals' *one more* deadly and invincible weapon.

Just about the only time many of us seem to overcome the *one-more* syndrome is when it comes to our faith lives. When was the last time we lingered after Mass for *one more* prayer? When was the last time we decided to attend Mass *one more* time during the week? Or when did we ever ask a parish committee if it could use *one more* volunteer to help in the church's ministry?

We can become so busy with the material *one mores* in our lives that we don't even think about the important spiritual *one mores*. How many of us, for example, will dig in our heels at the brink of death, pulling away as we plead for *one more* chance to develop a better prayer life, *one more* opportunity to perform an act of charity and justice, or *one more* try at being a good example to family and/or friends?

Epilogue

One night, caught in the vise between a particularly trying day at work and a potentially contentious school budget meeting that night, I yelled at the kids because they were bickering and making too much noise. Then I departed for the school-board meeting. While on the way I began to think about how I should summarize the reflections presented in this book.

I'd driven less than a block when it dawned on me that I couldn't very well come up with a way to drive home the messages in these anecdotes of faith until I really, *really* could act upon them myself, in my own home. I was missing the point when I lost my temper with the kids instead of resolving our tensions more peacefully. I'd forgotten again that they're walking, breathing, talking (sometimes noise-making) images of Christ, the greatest peacemaker. But I was warring against them because of that little bit of noise.

I realized then that I often write about how the kids inspire faith experiences in me and bring Christ into my life, but I often forget to give them the same message. I take the time and effort to tell perfect strangers about how meaningful the kids' actions are but forget to tell the kids themselves. I guess it's a lot easier — perhaps more human — to follow the yelling reflex when they act devilishly than it is to develop a hallelujah reflex for the times when they act angelically.

I think this idea had started forming as I was writing parts of this book because some of the chapters are revisions of columns I've written as managing editor of the *Catholic Bulletin* in St. Paul, Minnesota. Several times I discovered that columns I'd written three, six, or nine months before were tickling my conscience as I was revising them. Unfortunately, in some cases, I'd confined the thoughts to paper but forgot to carry them over into my daily life.

I'd written about the need to have more faith in the Son and in the sun but forgot to believe that when I ran into trouble on a cloudy day. I'd acknowledged that people are sacraments but failed to take the opportunity to thank them for that and experience their sacramentality more often. I'd preached that parents shouldn't be preoccupied with material things and housekeeping chores at the expense of spending time with their families, then turned around and painted a wall and put up a ceiling fan instead of going to the park for an afternoon in the sun.

The list is endless, and I can only hope that I'll get it right some day.

Some might wonder why I pulled all of these thoughts together if I'm still having so much trouble myself living them daily. After all, who am I to talk?

The answer is simple. I did so because I share the belief of many that we don't have to wait for Christ's Second Coming. He is here now in us, in our families and friends, and in strangers. He's even in our reflections on the little mysteries and awesome features of God's creation. Unfortunately, we often don't live like we believe that. Sometimes we get so crabby, surly, and cantankerous that it seems we've never even heard of the name Jesus Christ, except for its use as a swear word.

I share these stories not to draw attention to my own experiences. Rather, I'm trying to show how easily and frequently Christ can enter into simple events and relationships in life. I tell these tales with the wish that those who read them might find some spiritual or inspirational — or, sometimes at least, religiously entertaining — value in them. But most importantly, I write about my own revelations with the hope that those who read them might look for similar experiences in their own lives.

The presence of Christ, of God, is there in your life if you take the time to look, to listen, to feel. My experiences — and my struggles — might provide you with a shortcut, if you realize that the journey doesn't end with these experiences but only begins there. The secret is to experience them today and live them tomorrow and the next day and the next.

Obviously, I haven't acquired that knack yet. In part, that's why this isn't a how-to book in a market that abounds with such tomes. But I can guarantee you that it's worth the effort to seek out the meaning behind your experiences. Be yourself in doing so, because each person reflects on these experiences differently.

More on Everyday Spirituality from Liguori Publications

JESUS AS GIFT: Reflections on the Son
by Francis Quinlivan, C.S.C.

This book is a meditation on Jesus' promised gifts. Drawing on his own experience and the experiences of others, Father Quinlivan helps readers understand how they receive such gifts as the Holy Spirit, Peace, Rest, and many others. He explores their meaning in our lives and how these gifts can be sources of strength, encouragement, and hope. **$2.95**

FINDING GOD IN EVERYDAY LIFE
by Richard A. Boever, C.SS.R.

For those who may find true spirituality a confusing, elusive concept, this book offers a down-to-earth approach that helps readers discover how God works in their own lives and reveals how to live a fuller Christian life by responding to his call. **$1.95**

MORE GRAHAM CRACKERS, GALOSHES, AND GOD:
a second helping of laughs from everyday life, prayers for everyday problems
by Bernadette McCarver Snyder

Readers who enjoyed the first *Graham, Galoshes, and God* book kept telling us they wanted more! In this follow-up book, the author reveals how God always seems to show up in the midst of the frenzied furies and hilarious happenings in her housewifely life. Chapters include "Hazardous Happy Birthdays," "Do Angels Really Look Like Harpo Marx?" "The Inconvenience of Conveniences," "Wild Onions in the Garden of Life," and more. **$3.95**

Order from your local bookstore or write to:
Liguori Publications, Box 060, Liguori, Missouri 63057-9999
*(Please add $1.00 for postage and handling for orders under $5.00;
$1.50 for orders over $5.00.)*